No More

No Mas

"Saying no to negative mindsets by making positive confessions"

Robert & Dixie Summers

No More!

No Mas!

Published by

Summers Ministries

Columbus, Ohio

No More / No Mas©

Copyright 2018 by Summers Ministries, Inc.

All rights reserved

Unless otherwise indicated, all scriptures used are from the King James Version of the Bible

Printed in the USA

ISBN- 9781729252352

*"When Jesus saw that the people came running together, he rebuked the foul spirit, saying unto him, Thou dumb and deaf spirit, I charge thee, come out of him, and enter **no more** into him." – Mark 9:25*

Table of Contents

Introduction

Many people today suffer from a devaluation of self. Self is the real you. Self is not based on what you've accomplished in life, nor is it the mistakes you've made in life. Self is that unique and valuable person that God created you as. Self is not something or someone that you're striving to be. It is that which you are based on creation.

Large populations of people today have a low self-image. Much of this has been developed over time by the abuse, rejection and manipulation of others. It typically occurs early in life, specifically during the critical years of emotional development between 0 and 13 years old.

Perhaps you grew up in a family that was dysfunctional. While every family has some degree of dysfunction, it's when our original family members, comprised of mother, father and siblings are emotionally unhealthy that it can have lasting affect on our conscious and subconscious mind. Children that have been traumatized by family may carry emotional wounds throughout life. The five major areas of trauma to children are rejection, incest, molestation, emotional abuse and physical abuse.

Family environments lined with criticism, negative words, accusations, blame, violence, false responsibility, neglect and addictions are breeding grounds for the development of a devalued self.

Additionally, every child needs love, affirmation, attention, validation, protection, training and correction.

When we do not experience these basic traits we become insecure, unstable and have a sense of worthlessness. Over time, we can develop toxic thoughts about self and the world around us. These thoughts become ingrained in our subconscious mind and essentially guide our life. It's the perception you have about you that matters. Your perception is your reality. If you believe you are defective based on past experience or what someone did to you or said about you, that's who you become. The bible says, "as a man thinketh in his heart – so is he!"

If you've been around people that have been critical of you, devalued you or abused you, you may be emotionally scarred from these past wounds and as such, have a self-image of a discarded, ostracized and defective person. And while you can't change what people said or did to you, you can say "No More" to the emotional and mental soul-tie that exists.

It's time to come out of agreement with our past and align with who our creator says we are. Indeed it is a fact that things happened to us or that we did things that were evil. However, truth is greater than fact, and the truth is you are blameless in the sight of God. The truth is you have the mind of Christ. The truth is, you've been given everything you need that pertains to life and Godliness. Where is this truth? It's in you!

In Philemon 1:6 we are told to speak good things about ourselves. *"That the communication of thy faith may become effectual by the acknowledging of every good thing which is in you."* Do you know what's in you? Christ Jesus is in you!

What are you acknowledging about yourself? The bible says, "*out of the abundance of the heart the mouth will speak.*" Do you realize that your words are powerful? Yes, your words will shape your destiny and therefore affect your life whether positively or negatively. Therefore you should watch what you say. There is an old saying that confession brings possession. This is a true statement. That being so, we should make sure that what we say is what we want.

The moment you open your mouth and start speaking about the good things that are in you by Jesus Christ rather than circumstances or what someone else said about you, a supernatural connection is made between your faith and, the gifts, talents and destiny God has placed inside you. The confession of your mouth, your acknowledgement of the truth, is what ignites God's purpose and plan for your life.

We have designed this mini-book to be a resource for you as you start your journey into self-discovery of who you really are. The following declarations will change your life. You must agree with them as you say them. See yourself the way that God's word has told you that you are. Stop making wrong confessions that bring fear and doubt to your life. You were made in the image of God. He is a creator and he has made us like him with the ability to create. Use these words to create and shape your life and say NO MORE to the negative view of self.

No More Confessions

No more confessions are designed to '*draw a line in the sand*,' per se. They are representative of boundaries we are establishing in our lives. They are emphatic declarations and statements of power that demonic forces that have plagued us throughout life will no longer torment us. These confessions will emotionally and mentally liberate you from the lies the accuser has told you. When saying them, do so in a forceful, energetic and persuasive manner.

No More will I allow players, haters and manipulators to control my life.

No More will Satan control me, because I have been delivered from his power.

No More will I be a slave to the Flesh for I am NOW a servant of Christ.

No More will I allow the devil to do what he desires in my life, but I resist the devil, and he flees from me (James 4:7).

No More will I listen to or believe the lies of the devil, for he is a liar and the father of lies (John 8:44).

No More will I listen to the voice of the wicked one.

No More will I be vexed by unclean spirits (Luke 6:18).

No More will I be harassed by the enemy (Matt. 9:36).

No More will I be in bondage to anything, for Christ has made me free. (John 8:36)

No More will demons operate in and control my life.

No More will I allow the demons of fear to control my life.

No More will I allow the demons of pride to puff me up (1 Cor. 4:6).

No More will I allow the demons of lust to operate in my mind and body.

No More will I allow the demons of religion to make me act religiously.

No More will I allow the demons of double-mindedness to confuse me and make me indecisive (James 1:8).

No More will I allow the demons of rejection to control my life.

No More will I allow rebellion and disobedience to control my life.

No More will I allow curses to hinder my life. I break

every curse, for I have been redeemed from the curse (Gal. 3:13).

No More will I open the door for demons to come into my life through unforgiveness (Matt. 18:35).

No More will I open the door for demons to enter my life through habitual sin.

No More will I open the door for demons to enter my life through occult involvement.

No More will I open the door for demons to enter through the mind controlling tactics of Jezebel.

No More will the demon of mind control affect my thinking, I sever all the tentacles of mind control.

No More will serpent and scorpion spirits affect my life, for I have power to tread on serpents and scorpions.

No More will I allow demon spirits to torment and oppress me.

No More will the enemy be my master; Jesus is my Lord.

No More will I tolerate the works of the devil in my life, for Jesus came and destroyed the works of the devil (1 John 3:8).

No More will I allow passivity to keep me inactive.

No More will I be below and not above (Deut. 28:13).

No More will I be cursed and not walk in blessings, for the blessing of Abraham is mine (Gal 3:13-14).

No More will I say yes to the enemy.

No More will I agree to the lies of the devil.

No More will I compromise my standards and holiness; the Word of God is my standard, not the standards of the world (2 Cor. 10:2).

No More will I act hypocritically (Mark 7:6).

No More will I condemn the guiltless (Matt. 12:7).

No More will I give place to the devil (Eph. 4:27)

No More will I allow the enemy to control my will, but I submit my will to the will of God.

No More will I allow the enemy to control my emotions, but I yield my emotions to the joy and peace of God.

No More will I allow the enemy to control my sexual character, but I yield my body as a living sacrifice (Romans 12:1).

No More will I allow the enemy to control my mind, but I renew my mind with the Word of God (Romans 12:2).

No More will I allow the enemy to control my appetite, but I yield my appetite to the control of the Holy Spirit.

No More will I allow the enemy to control my tongue, but I yield my tongue to the Holy Spirit.

No More will I allow the enemy to control any part of my life, but my life is fully submitted to the Holy Spirit and Word of God.

No More will I allow the enemy to control my destiny, but God is the author, revealer and finisher of my destiny.

No More will I allow the enemy to abort the plan of God for my life.

No More will I allow people to draw me away from the love of God, but I commit myself to walking in love, for God is love (1 John 4:7-8).

No More will I shut up the bowels of compassion (1 John 3:17).

No More will I behave unseemly, for love does not behave unseemly (1 Cor. 13:5).

No More will I be easily provoked, for love is not easily provoked (1 Cor. 13:5).

No More will I seek my own, for love does not seek its own (1 Cor. 13:5).

No More will I think evil, for love does not think evil (1 Cor. 13:5).

No More will I lose hope, for love hopes for all things (1 Cor. 13:7).

No More will I give up, for love endures all things (1 Cor. 13:7).

No More will I act and think like a child (1 Cor. 13:11).

No More will I be passive with the gifts of the Spirit, but I desire the spiritual gifts to operate in my life. (1 Cor. 14:1).

No More will I allow the accuser to accuse me, for I am washed and cleansed by the blood of the Lamb (Rev 1:5; 7:14).

No More will I labor and work in vain (Isaiah 65:23).

No More will the heavens be shut over my life, but the Lord has opened the windows of heaven (Malachi 3:10).

I AM Confessions

I AM confessions remind you of who you are In-Christ. This is your true identity. It's what God has said about you – His creation. Challenge yourself to repeat them for at least 30 days. Believe the words you speak and see the dramatic change that they bring to your life.

I am a Child of God (Romans 8:16)

I am Redeemed from the hand of the enemy (Psalms 107:2)

I am Forgiven (Colossians 1:13-24)

I am Saved by grace through faith (Ephesians 2:8)

I am Justified (Romans 5:1)

I am Sanctified (1st Corinthians 6:11)

I am A new creature (2nd Corinthians 5:17)

I am A partaker of His divine nature (1st Peter 1:4)

I am Redeemed from the curse of the law (Galatians 3:13)

I am Delivered from the power of darkness (Colossians 1:13)

I am Led by the Spirit of God (Romans 8:14)

I am A son of God (Roman 8:14)

I am Kept in safety wherever I go (Psalms 91:11)

I am Getting all my needs met by Jesus (Philippians 4:19)

I am Casting all my cares of Jesus (1st Peter 5:7)

I am Strong in the Lord and in the Power of His might (Ephesians 6:10)

I am Doing all things through Christ that strengthens me (Philippians 4:13)

I am An heir of God and joint heir with Jesus (Romans 8:17)

I am Heir to the blessings of Abraham (Galatians 3:13-14)

I am Observing and obeying all the commandments of the Lord (Deuteronomy 28:12)

I am Blessed coming in and going out (Deuteronomy 28:6)

I am An inheritor of Eternal life (1st John 5:11-12)

I am Blessed with all spiritual blessings (Ephesians 1:3)

I am Healed by the stripes of Jesus (1st Peter 2:24)

I am Exercising my authority over the enemy (Luke 10:19)

I am Above and not beneath (Deuteronomy 28:13)

I am More than a conqueror (Romans 8:37)

I am Establishing God's word here on the earth (Matthew 16:19)

I am An overcomer by the blood of the Lamb and the word of my Testimony (Revelation 12:11)

I am Daily overcoming the devil (1st John 4:4)

I am not weighed down by depression.

I am Not moved by what I see (2nd Corinthians 4:18)

I am Walking by faith and not by sight (2nd Corinthians 5:7)

I am Casting down vain imaginations (2nd Corinthians 10:4-5)

I am Bringing every thought into captivity (2nd Corinthians 10:5)

I am Being transformed by the renewing of my mind (Romans 12:1-2)

I am A laborer together with God in Christ (2nd Corinthians 3:9)

I am The righteousness of God in Christ ((2nd Corinthians 5:21)

I am An imitator of Jesus (Ephesians 5:1)

I am The light of the World (Matthew 5:14)

Confessions when you wake up

It's time to stop listening to the devil and to your own negative thoughts. Start your day by conditioning your mind to command your life to go in the direction you want. Realize how much power resides in your mouth and position yourself for a productive, prosperous and purposeful day.

My mind is rested.

My mind is reset.

My mind is sharp.

My thinking is not dull.

I have a sound mind.

I possess brilliance.

My mind thinks clearly today.

I will not be confused.

I am single minded.

I am decisive.

I have a ready mind.

I have a pure mind.

I have a peaceful mind.

I have a willing mind.

I do not worry.

I am not anxious.

I am not fearful.

I am in my right mind.

I have the mind of Christ.

God's laws are in my mind.

My mind is renewed.

I think godly thoughts.

I gird up the loins of my mind.

My mind stays on the Lord.

The Lord keeps my mind.

I am spiritually minded.

I mind the things of the Spirit.

My flesh does not control my mind.

My mind is not puffed up.

I walk with humbleness of mind.

I do not think vain thoughts.

I think soberly.

I think creatively.

I have inspired thoughts.

My brain functions at optimum level.

Every part of my brain functions properly.

Blood flows to my brain properly.

My mind will not be blocked.

My mind will not be tormented.

I have a great memory.

My thoughts are established.

My mind is anointed.

I have the spirit of knowledge.

I have the spirit of wisdom.

I have the spirit of understanding.

My meditation will be sweet.

I have a wealth mentality.

My mind prospers.

I do not have a poverty mentality.

I have a prosperity mentality.

My mind will not doubt.

My mind will not drift.

Self-Affirmations

Affirmations help purify our thoughts and rewire the dynamics of our brains so that we truly begin to think nothing is impossible. Life and death are in the power of the tongue. Use God's word to bring His power and blessing into your life.

Affirmations strengthen us by helping us believe in the potential of an action we desire to manifest. When we verbally affirm our dreams and ambitions, we are instantly empowered with a broad sense of reassurance that our wishful words will become a reality.

Say the following (I can / I am / I have) affirmations out loud:

I am valuable.

I can be myself and honor the uniqueness of others.

I have a positive outlook on life.

I can be independent and interdependent.

I can love others unconditionally and accept them for who they are.

I can finish each part of life's journey and look forward to the next adventure.

I can be creative, competent, productive and joyful.

I can be a responsible, punctual, and dependable person.

I can be accountable for my contributions to each of my commitments in life.

I can embrace people, my role, my dreams and my decisions.

I am lovable at my present age.

I can love my neighbor, my family and myself

I am not afraid of loving those that hurt me.

I have many talents, and I use them effectively.

I can be generous and share with those in need.

I can celebrate the gifts given to me.

I can abandon my old habits and take up new, more positive ones.

I am deserving of the support that I need.

I can let go of fear.

I am superior to negative thoughts and childish behaviors.

I forgive those who have harmed me in my past and can peacefully detach from them.

I am flowing with compassion that washes away my anger and replaces it with love.

I am led by the Holy Spirit towards my destiny.

I am courageous, and I am capable of standing up for myself.

I am at peace with all that has happened, is happening, and will happen.

I can look forward to what lies ahead, for everyday is a new day.

I refuse to dwell on past hurts and mistakes.

I can forgive those that wronged me.

I can set boundaries in my life without fear of rejection by others.

I am not yet the person I am capable of being and fully intend to be, but I am working diligently to become that person God has ordained me to be.

I am not depressed for it has no place in me and I refuse to accept it.

I can encourage myself.

I do not have to feel guilty or condemned just because someone else does not agree with me or doesn't like something I said, did or how I feel.

I have the right to say "no" without feeling guilty.

I have the right to ask questions.

I have the right to say I don't understand without feeling interior or stupid.

I don't have to apologize for saying no.

I don't have to apologize for making decisions that goes against others, including my friends, my family, my spouse and society.

I can be angry and express it in a responsible manner.

I have the right and responsibility to establish boundaries in my life.

I don't need to apologize for setting boundaries.

I don't need to have permission to set boundaries.

I have the right and responsibility to communicate my boundaries in a clear and consistent manner.

I can tell others what I'm not comfortable with.

I have the right to not take on the responsibilities of others.

I have the right to ask others for help.

I have the right to tell others when I feel they're manipulating, controlling, intimidating or dominating me.

I have the right to separate from abusive relationships.

I have the right to freely choose who I associate with.

I have a right to live healthy.

I do not need to lower my standards of living for others.

I have the right to make mistakes and learn from them.

I have the right to be myself.

I don't need the approval of others for the things I say, do or think.

I refuse to be blamed.

I have the right to change my mind.

I have the right and responsibility to divest from toxic relationships.

I am not defined by what others say about me.

I am not defined by my past. I can receive correction openly and reject criticism emphatically.

Daily Confessions for a Victorious Life

Many people are living defeated, unproductive and unsatisfactory lives. They have never experience the peaceful, joyous, prosperous and abundant life. God wants you to life a victorious life. The word of God says, *"Beloved, I wish above all things that thou mayest prosper and be in health, even as thy soul prospereth."* (3 John 1:2).

I John 5:4-5 states, *"For whatsoever is born of God overcometh the world: and this is the victory that overcometh the world, even our faith. Who is he that overcometh the world, but he that believeth that Jesus is the Son of God."* Do you believe Jesus is the Son of God? If so, then you are an overcomer. However, to experience this you must speak and use faith. Faith is expressed by the words of our mouth. Faith speaks!

The following confessions are designed to help you see yourself victorious in life.

I have no worries for I cast all of my cares over on Jesus, for He cares for me.

I have no heavy burdens because I've taken Jesus' yoke, which is easy, and His burden, which is light.

I am the body of Christ so Satan has no power over me and I overcome evil with good.

No weapon formed against me shall prosper, for my righteousness is of the Lord.

Whatever I do will prosper for I'm like a tree that's planted by the rivers of water.

My God will meet all my needs according to His riches in glory in Christ Jesus.

I am of (from) God and have overcome Satan, because the one who is in me is greater than the one who is in the world.

Christ has redeemed me from the curse of the law. Therefore, I forbid any sickness or disease to come upon this body. Every disease germ and every virus that touches this body dies instantly in the name of Jesus. Every organ and every tissue of this body functions in the perfection to which God created it to function. And I forbid any malfunction in this body, in the name of Jesus.

I am an overcomer and I overcome by the blood of the lamb and the word of my testimony.

The devil flees from me because I resist him in the name of Jesus.

The Word of God is forever settled in heaven. Therefore, I establish His Word upon this earth.

I have great peace because I am taught of the Lord.

No weapon formed against me shall prosper, and every controlling tongue that rises against me shall be found to be in the wrong.

I will not allow my soul to be cast down for I put my hope and trust in God.

I am above only and not beneath. I am the head and not the tail. I'm blessed coming in and blessed going out.

I am one spirit with God and I abide in Him always.

I have the mind of Jesus Christ and the wisdom of God flows in me and through me.

In my pathway of life, there is no death.

My body is the temple of God the Father, the Son and the Holy Spirit, for the fullness of God dwells in me.

I tread upon serpents and scorpions and I exercise righteous authority over all the power of the enemy. Nothing shall by any means hurt me.

I am trained in the word of righteousness and I call things that be not as though they were.

I will not fear what man shall do me because no weapon formed against me shall prosper..

Christ has not given me the spirit of fear but of power, love and a sound mind.

The blood of the Lord Jesus Christ covers my spirit, soul and body, and has sanctified me and separated me from the world, the flesh and the devil.

I not only have my senses exercised to discern both good and evil, but I aggressively come against the kingdom of darkness and spoil every plot and scheme Satan has waged against me and those around me.

I am more than a conqueror through Jesus Christ.

I take my shield of faith and quench Satan's fiery darts.

I will not be distracted from doing the will of God, and I will not stray to the left hand or to the right.

I place my hands on the plow of the Kingdom and will never look back at religion.

I have sound judgment and discretion and I refuse to be deceived by Satan in any way.

My mind is sharp and my spirit is acutely sensitive to disturbances in the spirit realm.

I watch and pray and prevent myself from being tempted by the enemy.

I am equipped with spiritual covering and weaponry and I am never caught off guard by the wicked one.

I've been made righteous and will never back down from the truth.

I am bold as a lion and I refuse to be intimidated by the enemy.

I exercise dominion over the earth.

I reign in life by Jesus Christ through grace and righteousness.

My love casts out fear and I aggressively love others unconditionally. For love never fails.

All of my days are filled with abundance, prosperity and peace, because Jesus is Lord over my life.

I choose to be a vessel through which His will can be done in the earth.

The Kingdom of God rules over all, and the Kingdom is within me.

I will fear no evil, for you are with me Lord; Your Word and Your Spirit they comfort me.

I am far from oppression, and fear does not come near me.

I am delivered from the evil of this present world, for this is the will of God.

I am a doer of the Word of God and I am blessed in my deeds.

I take the shield of faith and quench every fiery dart that the wicked one brings against me.

My body is the house of God. God lives big in me and I belong to Him. I've been bought with the price of the blood of Jesus.

I glorify God in my body, my mind and in my spirit.

Satan has no power over me. I have been delivered from the power of darkness and translated into the Kingdom of God's dear Son. Therefore sin has no dominion over me.

Every place I go, the Kingdom of God goes, for His Kingdom is in me.

I separate myself from every unclean thing.

I submit myself to God. I resist the devil and he flees from me.

I give no place or no opportunity to the devil.

I choose the fear of the Lord, which is to hate evil, pride, arrogance, the evil way, and the disobedient mouth.

I consider Jesus and His presence in me.

I love God more than anything this world offers.

I present my body as a living sacrifice to God - holy, devoted, and consecrated to please Him, which is a part of my spiritual worship to Him.

I am not conformed to this world's way of thinking, but I am being transformed by the renewing of my mind to His Word so that I can prove what is the good, the acceptable, and the perfect will of God in my life.

I have the mind of Christ and know all things.

Jesus said, "The prince of the world comes, but he has nothing in Me." Therefore, I decree that Satan has nothing in me.

I cast down imaginations and every thought that tries to exalt itself against the knowledge of God. I bring my thoughts into captivity to the obedience of Christ and His Word - having a ready mind to revenge all disobedience.

I think on things that are true, honest, just, pure, lovely, and of good report. If there be any virtue or praise, these are the things I think on.

In righteousness I am established. I am far from oppression. I do not fear. I am far from terror. It will not come near me.

Thy Word have I hid in my heart that I might not sin against God.

If I sin, God is faithful and just to forgive me of it and to cleanse me from all unrighteousness.

No weapon formed against me shall prosper and every tongue that rises against me is condemned or shown to be wrong and stopped. This is the heritage God has given me as a servant of the Lord and my righteousness is of Him.

I love righteousness and I hate iniquity; therefore God anoints me with the oil of gladness.

Lord, You said there is no temptation that has come to me or that can come to me that is not common to man, or beyond human resistance. I will not be tempted beyond my strength to resist, God you promised that you would provide a way out or a way of escape so I will be strong against it.

I am of God and I have overcome every anti-Christ spirit because greater is He who is in me than he who is in the world.

This is the victory that causes me to overcome in this world - my faith in Jesus the King and in His Word.

I live and walk by faith and not by sight, feelings or my emotions.

I live by every Word that proceeds from the mouth of God.

I let the Word of Christ dwell in me richly in all wisdom.

I believe and therefore I speak.

I overcome the devil by the blood of the Lamb and by the word of my testimony, not loving my life unto the death.

I shall live and not die.

All things are working together for good in my life because I love God and I am called according to His purpose.

I thank my God who gives me the victory through my Lord and King Jesus. He always causes me to triumph.

I can do all things through Christ who strengthens me.

Confessions that bring Increase, Wealth and Prosperity

Poverty and lack are a condition of one's mindset. Many struggle with seeing themselves as ever having wealth or provision to enjoy life. Others have difficulty starting businesses or succumb to a lifetime of defeat and depression in the area of finances. These confessions are designed to help condition your mind for the life you desire to live.

God has blessed me abundantly and I am a blessing. (Genesis 12:2)

The Lord makes all that I do prosper in my hand. (Genesis 39:3)

Because the Lord is with me, all that I do prospers greatly. (Genesis 39:23)

The Lord delights in me, he has brought me into a land that flows with milk and honey. (Numbers 14:8)

For the Lord my God has blessed me greatly in all the works of my hand. (Deuteronomy 2:7)

God is faithful; he keeps his covenant and mercy to them that love him. (Deuteronomy 7:9)

God loves me, blesses me and multiplies me abundantly (Deuteronomy 7:13)

I am blessed above all people. (Deuteronomy 7:14)

God has brought me into a good abundant land; I eat without scarceness and do not lack any good thing. (Deuteronomy 8:6-9)

God has given me the power to get wealth so his covenant is established in the earth. (Deuteronomy 8:18)

I rejoice in all I put my hand to because God has blessed me greatly. (Deuteronomy 12:7)

God has blessed me and he promised me that I would lend to many and not borrow. (Deuteronomy 15:6)

God has brought me into this place; he has given me this land that flows abundantly with milk and honey. (Deuteronomy 26:9)

All the blessings of Abraham have come on me in abundance and overtaken me. (Deuteronomy 28:2)

I am blessed in the city and in my country.

My children are blessed.

The increase of my ground is blessed.

All my methods of transportation are blessed.

My checking, savings and investment accounts are blessed.

I am blessed when I rise and when I sleep.

I am blessed when I come in and when I go out. (Deuteronomy 28:3-6)

The Lord has commanded the blessing on my storehouse and me and on all I set my hands to do. He has blessed me abundantly in this land. (Deuteronomy 28:8)

God has made me plentiful in goods, cattle, and the fruit of my body and ground. (Deuteronomy 28:11)

God has opened unto me his good treasure to give rain to my land and bless all the work of my hand. I will lend and not borrow. (Deuteronomy 28:12)

I am the head and not the tail, I am above and not beneath. (Deuteronomy 28:13)

I keep the words of Gods covenant and I do them, I prosper in all that I do. (Deuteronomy 29:9)

God has made me plenteous in every good work of my hand, in the fruit of my body, cattle and land, for good and he rejoices over me. (Deuteronomy 30:9)

God has set this day before me and I choose life and abundance. (Deuteronomy 30:15-16)

I am strong and very courageous, I turn not to the right or the left, and I prosper wherever I go. (Joshua 1:7)

The word makes my way prosperous and makes me abundantly successful. (Joshua 1:8)

The Lord makes me abundantly rich and lifts me up. (1 Samuel 2:7)

I keep the word and I prosper in all I do. (1 Kings 2:3)

Wisdom and knowledge is granted to me and God gives me riches, wealth and honor in abundance. (2 Chronicles 1:12)

I believe God's word spoken by His prophets and I prosper. (2 Chronicles 20:20)

As long as I seek after the Lord and His Kingdom he makes me prosperous. (2 Chronicles 26:5, Matthew 6:33)

I lay up gold as dust and have plenty of silver because I have delighted in the Almighty. (Job 22:24-25)

I obey and serve God and I spend my days in prosperity and my years in pleasure. (Job 36:11)

I am blessed because I walk not in the counsel of the ungodly, but I delight in the law of the Lord. (Psalm 1:1-2)

I am like a tree planted by the rivers of water, I bring forth my fruit in season, my leaf does not wither and everything I do prospers abundantly. (Psalm 1:3)

The Lord blesses me and his favor is around me like a shield. (Psalm 5:12)

The Lord is my shepherd therefore I am not in want, I am walking in abundance. (Psalm 23:1)

Goodness and mercy follow me all the days of my life. (Psalm 23:6)

Because I seek the Lord I do not lack any good thing. (Psalm 34:10)

Let the Lord be magnified who takes pleasure in my abundant prosperity. (Psalm 35:27)

I delight myself in the Lord and he gives me the desires of my heart. (Psalm 37:4)

I am abundantly blessed because I trust in the Lord. (Psalm 40:4)

God has brought me into a wealthy place. (Psalm 66:12)

God heaps his abundant benefits on me. (Psalm 68:19)

I am blessed because my strength is in the Lord. (Psalm 84:5)

I am blessed because I dwell in the house of the Lord. (Psalm 84:4)

The Lord has given me that which is good and my land yields it's increase. (Psalm 85:12)

God has increased me mightily and made me stronger than my doubters. (Psalm 105:24)

God has brought me forth with silver and gold. (Psalm 105:37)

I am blessed because I fear the Lord and delight greatly in his commandments. (Psalm 112:1)

Wealth and riches are in my house. (Psalm 112:3)

God blesses them that fear him both small and great. (Psalm 115:13)

The Lord has increased me more and more, me and my children. (Psalm 115:14)

The Lord has dealt bountifully with me. (Psalm 116:7)

Thank you Lord for sending prosperity now. (Psalm 118:25)

I am blessed because I keep his testimonies and seek him with my whole heart. (Psalm 119:2)

Peace is within my walls and prosperity in my home. (Psalm 122:7)

I am blessed because I fear the Lord and walk in his ways. (Psalm 128:1)

I eat the labor of my hands and it is well with me and I am happy. (Psalm 128:2)

I honor the Lord with my substance and first fruits of my increase, my barns are filled with plenty and my vats are bursting forth with new wine. (Proverbs 3:9-10)

God blesses my habitation. (Proverbs 3:33)

God causes me to inherit substance and he fills my treasure. (Proverbs 8:21)

The blessing of the Lord makes me rich and he adds no sorrow with it. (Proverbs 10:22)

My hands are diligent and it makes me rich. (Proverbs 10:4)

Blessings are upon my head and my memory is blessed. (Proverbs 10:6-7)

A gracious woman preserves her honor and strong men maintain riches. (Proverbs 11:16)

I am generous and I prosper, I rejuvenate others and I myself am rejuvenated. (Proverbs 11:25)

He that gathers by labor shall increase. (Proverbs 13:11)

The wealth of the wicked is laid up for me and it is coming to me now in overflowing proportions. (Proverbs 13:22)

In my house are many treasures because I am in right standing with the Lord. (Proverbs 15:6)

I commit my works to the Lord and my thoughts are established. (Proverbs 16:3)

Through wisdom my house is constructed and by understanding it is established and by knowledge the cracks are filled with all good and pleasant riches. (Proverbs 24:3-4)

I am faithful and I overflow with blessings. (Proverbs 28:20)

I put my trust in the Lord and I am blessed and developed. (Proverbs 28:25)

I am willing and obedient and I eat the good of the land. (Isaiah 1:19)

The Lord teaches me to profit and leads me in the way I should go. (Isaiah 48:17)

I eat the wealth of the nations. (Isaiah 61:6)

God has prospered me and given me hope and a great future. (Jeremiah 29:11)

God has enriched me with a host of riches and his merchandise. (Ezekiel 27:33)

My posterity is prosperous and my investments yield fruit. (Zechariah 8:12)

The wealth of the heathen is gathered together in abundance for me, gold, silver and apparel are in great supply. (Zechariah 14:14)

God has opened the hatchways of heaven above me and is pouring out a continuous blessing upon me, so much that I am brimming with plenty. (Malachi 3:10)

All the nations of the earth call me blessed. (Malachi 3:12)

God has given me this day my daily sustenance, He leads me beside still waters and restores my soul. (Matthew 6:11)

I am increasing in wisdom and favor with God and man. (Luke 2:52)

I have given and it is given unto me, good measure, pressed down, shaken together, and running over do men give into my bosom. For with the same measure I give it is given back to me in bursting abundance. (Luke 6:38)

Jesus came that I have life and have it more abundantly. (John 10:10)

There are none around me that lack any good thing. (Acts 4:34)

I owe no man anything but to love him. (Romans 13:8)

I sow bountifully and I reap bountifully. (2 Corinthians 9:6)

God has made all grace abound toward me so that I having all sufficiency in all things do abound to every good work. (2 Corinthians 9:8)

I have been made rich in every way so that I can be generous on every occasion and through this God gets the glory. (2 Corinthians 9:11)

The blessings of Abraham have come on me through Jesus. (Galatians 3:14)

I will not be deceived, nor do I mock God, for whatsoever I sow I also reap. (Galatians 6:7)

God is able to do exceeding abundantly above all that I ask or think, according to the power that works in me. (Ephesians 3:20)

My God supplies all my need according to his riches in glory by Christ Jesus. (Philippians 4:19)

I will not be high-minded, or trust in uncertain riches, but in God who gives me all things to enjoy. (1 Timothy 6:17)

I am rich in good works, ready to distribute and willing to share. (1 Timothy 6:18

Every good and perfect gift I receive comes from my Father in heaven. James 1:17)

I prosper and am in health even as my soul prospers. (3 John 1:2)

Confessions for a Healthy Marriage

Marriage is an awesome institution ordained by God and it should be a blessing. However, so many are challenged, frustrated and feel hopeless in their current relationship. It's time to roll up your sleeves, get in the fight and take back your marriage. Stop allowing the enemy to use your mouth as a tool for his destruction. Begin to speak life into your marriage. Commit your mouth to be a well of life by releasing these dynamic confessions of faith over your marriage. Remember, you have dominion and authority.

I receive and release strength, honor, and glory that marriage brings in Jesus name.

I decree and declare that my marriage shall reflect the glory of God in Jesus name.

I decree and declare that two shall put to flight ten thousand.

I decree and declare that cycles of dysfunctional marriages in my bloodline are broken in the name of Jesus.

All words of witchcraft spoken against my marriage are rendered powerless in Jesus name.

I position sentinels along my marriage to protect it from that which would look to divide.

The word of God surrounds my marriage in the name of Jesus.

The word of the Lord is a strong tower in my marriage.

I establish boundaries in my marriage; for it shall not be like a city with no walls.

I decree and declare that I will have prophetic announcements over my marriage in Jesus name.

The Word of God is the foundation of my marriage and I align it to the word of God in the name of Jesus.

I raise the banner and the standard of Christ and declare the Lordship of Jesus over my marriage in Jesus name.

I decree and declare that my marriage shall bear good fruits in Jesus name.

Every spirit of unproductiveness in my marriage is broken, and rooted out in the name of Jesus.

All pain and suffering is removed from my marriage, in Jesus name.

I removed the spirit of unforgiveness, bitterness and retaliation from my marriage in Jesus name.

I release the word of God into every area of my marriage where wounds are decaying.

I (we) rebuke the spirit of rage, violence, hatred and abuse from my (our) marriage in Jesus name.

I decree and declare that the aroma of my marriage is a pleasing aroma in your sight Lord.

I declare that my marriage is a testimony of Jesus' love relationship He has with His bride, the body of Christ.

I decree and declare that every dry area in my marriage becomes saturated with the presence of God.

My marriage is resurrected by the power of God. I speak life to every dead area in my marriage in Jesus name.

I release every good thing in my marriage in Jesus name.

Let every outsider that has invaded my marriage be removed in Jesus name.

Let every sower of discord in my marriage be exposed.

Let every demonic voice that's infiltrated my marriage be muzzled.

Let every well of perversion in my marriage be dried up.

Let every gate of confusion in my marriage be broken.

Let all prophetic witchcraft and the sorcerers tongue be put to death in my marriage.

Let the spirit of adultery be removed from my marriage.

I extinguish every lying tongue against my marriage in Jesus name.

I remove all oppression, stress and strife from my marriage in Jesus name.

I uproot every demonic seed plated in my marriage.

I break every soul tie with former lovers and spouses in Jesus name.

I decree and declare that the bars of my marriage gates will be strengthened in the name of Jesus.

I sever all confederacies, contracts, agreements, alliances and soul ties with Jezebel and command her to be removed from my marriage in Jesus name.

I resist the spirit of accusation from having a part in my marriage.

I speak healing, restoration, love, revival, joy, peace, favor, harmony, unity, wisdom, understanding, knowledge, fruitfulness, increase, excitement, fire, prosperity, wholeness into my marriage.

Prayer for Marriages
(to be prayed together as a married couple)

Father God, we lift our marriage up to you. We understand that our union together is a picture of our relationship with Christ. We direct our thoughts about each other to be in agreement with your will and we are committed to having a successful marriage relationship.

We agree to be kind, tenderhearted, respectful and patient toward each other according to your word, forgiving each other, regardless of the situation. We will not curse but bless one another. We choose to speak the truth in love and listen well to each other. We choose to speak life into our marriage relationship and dedicate ourselves to encouraging each other.

Lord, we need your help, strength and direction. Help us to pray together, to trust in you and walk in obedience to your word so that we may have peace, joy and prosperity in our marriage. Let your love be the example on how we should love each other. Teach (husband) how to love (wife) like Christ loves the church, and teach (wife) to honor and respect (husband).

Forgive us for any anger, blame, accusation and control that we may have displayed towards each other. Give us your wisdom and guidance while we work on ourselves. Help us to see you as our source of acceptance, healing, validation and affirmation.

Bring deliverance to our lives and heal those areas of brokenness and pain. Deliver us from rejection, insecurity, withdrawal, abandonment and suspicion. Let us extend mercy to each other, forgiving each other daily. Let us bless and curse not.

Lord Jesus, today we choose to be transparent to each other and confess our shortcomings openly to each other so we can receive your healing. We receive your love, forgiveness, acceptance, favor, harmony, unity, truth, patience, kindness, joy, faithfulness and self-control into our individual lives and marriage relationship.

We commit this day that our bodies are not our own—that they belong to each other and to you. We choose not to deprive each other of sexual love and to remain faithful to each other only. We openly confess to each other that we will honor, respect, encourage and bless each other. We will not abuse, manipulate, control, dominate or intimidate each other.

Father, we ask that you remove the scales from our eyes so that we can see the truth of what marriage is and the responsibilities we have to each other, and so that we can create a loving partnership of commitment, trust and understanding. We resist the enemy that would attempt to destroy our marriage. We bind, sever, break and destroy every demonic principality, power and ruler of the darkness of this world from having part in our relationship to each other. We command the ancient spirit of Jezebel tied to divorce, division, seduction, judgment, criticism, addiction, control, self-pity, hatred, lying and deception to be removed from our marriage now!

We uproot every evil word spoken against each other and cast down every vain imagination we have towards each other. We forgive each other for past offenses. We renounce all soul-ties with the past and look forward to a new life together.

Lord, we agree that will only look to your counsel surrounding our marriage. We desire only to allow friends, family, church family and leaders into our life that value marriage and your word. We remove ourselves from those who would seduce us, divide us, lie to us and bring discord in our marriage.

We understand that we are heirs together in the grace of life and remain faithful to each other. We will prevail in every situation, circumstance, trial and test. We will never give up! We look forward to growing, maturing and developing into the couple you desire us to be. We desire your will, not ours. We ask that your Holy Spirit do a mighty work in our marriage. We submit our marriage and individual lives to you. Have your way Lord! We know that you are for us, and therefore who can be against us?

In Jesus Name

Confessions for the Unmarried
(Those who desire to be married)

Although there is nothing wrong with remaining unmarried, many desire to become married at some point in their life. Marriage is an honorable thing and God's Word does promise you a spouse of your own if you want one. We should never rush into marriage. However if you desire to have a spouse there are things you can do now to create the environment for a healthy person to come into your life. Others who are 'waiting' for the right person to cross their path can get weary, even discouraged while waiting. Rather than being passive, frustrated or giving up, you can begin calling things into existence and contend with any evil forces that are blocking you from being married.

The following declarations, decrees and confessions of faith will assist you in achieving the desire of your heart.

I call forth my marriage partner in the name of Jesus.

Let every deaf and dumb spirit that causes me not to see my spouse be destroyed by the hammer of God.

Let every deaf and dumb spirit that causes my spouse not to see me be destroyed by the thunder of God.

Father, cleanse my eyes with your eye balm that I may see my partner in the name of Jesus.

Every wicked view I've had regarding my marital status be wiped-out by the blood of Jesus.

Let every strongman and stronghold in my life that would hinder me from being married be discovered in Jesus name.

Let every wicked altar that's been erected in my life be pulverized by the axe of the Lord.

Let every negative thought that would cause me to doubt my ability to attract and discover my future spouse be silenced by the voice of Lord.

I declare that I shall enter into marriage at the perfect timing of the Holy Spirit.

I release my spouse from the imprisonment of the enemy and remove every shackle and heavy weight that would hinder our paths from crossing.

God is preparing the perfect mate for me, and when the Spirit of God causes our paths to cross, I have favor in his/her eyes.

Father, guide me to the person who is right for me. Guide me to someone who loves you above all things.

I remove every active evil pattern in my life that would hinder me from getting married.

I remove every generational curse tied to my bloodline in the area of establishing a healthy relationship and marriage in the name of Jesus.

Holy Spirit let your power; your majesty, your authority and your dominion sit at the gate of my life.

Let every word curse spoken against my life that would hinder me from attracting a healthy mate be broke in Jesus name.

I declare my mind and emotions are healed from all wounds and hurts from prior relationships.

I broke every soul tie with former lovers that would keep me from my future spouse in Jesus name.

I command every sexually transmitted demon that infected my mind, emotions and body to be removed from now, in Jesus name.

I choose to keep myself sanctified until marriage.

Let every wicked contract and agreement that I made with doubt, fear, unforgiveness and bitterness be broken.

Let every negative word that I've spoken against men (women) be uprooted in Jesus name.

I declare that I am valuable and worthy to be loved by my future spouse.

I uphold a high standard for my life and only attract potential spouses that value and respect me.

I resist all temptation to settle for less than what I'm worthy to have.

I deserve only the best and desire a spouse that loves me, values me and wants the best for me.

I have the right to love my future spouse without fear of rejection.

I respect myself and demand respect by others.

My body is the temple of the Holy Spirit and it is reserved solely for my future spouse.

I have discernment and wisdom to guard my heart from those who do not value me as the person I now am.

I desire to have a husband or wife of my own, and it is God's will to give me one.

Other Books by Robert & Dixie Summers

Deliverance Training Manual - 101©

It's about Time

Genuine Fathers – Willing Sons ©

Kingdom Principles of Success, Wealth & Prosperity ©

Harboring the Spirit of Jezebel ©

Gossip – The Weapon of Mass Destruction ©

Throw Jezebel Down ©

Jezebels Whoredoms, Perversions and Witchcrafts ©

Deliverance Training Manual 201 ©

The Petrified Soul ©

For more information please visit
www.summersministries.com

Made in the USA
Lexington, KY
26 November 2019